Navigating the River of Aging

Live life with zest!

Marilyn Stuby

Marilyn Slaby is author of Marilyn's Ginger 'n' Jazz,
Quick and Healthy Recipes (1991)

ISBN 978-0-9837480-0-7

Graphic design by Anne McKinney
Photographs by Marilyn Slaby

Navigating the River of Aging
By
Marilyn Slaby

Dedicated to the clients I have come to know and love – in the past, in the present, and in the future. My life has a richness it would not have had without you. You are forever in my heart.

Table of Contents

Acknowledgement

Our time on this earth feels short and very precious. Many heartfelt thanks to all who encourage me and listen to my wild plans and notions. Your gifts of time and friendship feel like a warm hug to me. My sweet mother, Audrey Pittenger, you continue to be such a doll! Thanks for reading and editing for me and for being the woman I turn to most in life. Your steady confidence, love and belief in me feel superb. Thank you, Bonnie Nester, author of Moments this Good, for your kind guidance, wonderful comments, and eagerness to edit my book. Carolyn Pittenger, sister, thanks for helping me in a pinch by suggesting "just one more thing." The book is better. Karen Truax, sister to me in our favorite field, thanks for your insightful comments.

Mom and Dad, you have continued to be there for each of your children; we have much to be grateful for in the way we were raised. Mike, one of the reasons I married you was because you offer support when I doubt, you encourage when I feel disheartened, and you grin when I take myself too seriously. Matthew and Monica, your dedicated love, enthusiasm, your pride in me, warm my soul.

All names in my book have been changed, as I would never wish to breach any of my client's privacy. Any similarities between my clients and someone you know are strictly coincidental.

Forward

As I look ahead in this decade, like you, I will come a little closer to the "aged" me. Of course, it's a big secret. Baby boomers are not going to get old... I've seen enough to know there is work to do to make these exciting years powerful and enduring. I have much to share with you. I focus on several topics that help us expand our understanding of what will be required for us to enjoy the process of aging as much as possible. Boomers will demand more services, better care, and an overall better quality of life. Our parents will benefit from the knowledge we gain as we help them determine what solutions work for everyone.

Introduction

A client told me the only thing golden about the golden years is the color of your pee. How's *that* for making you want to embrace old age? Let's talk.

By now, you've heard baby boomers are ready to take over the country! Okay – maybe not, but we *are* the largest growing segment of the population. We represent changing attitudes and the determination to deal with the transitions of aging with panache and verve, not only for ourselves, but also for our aging parents. We are the sandwich generation. Like every generation, we find ourselves pulled in many directions, as we deal with the demands of our adult children, sometimes grandchildren, and the needs of our parents.

In the years since I started *There For You*, I've had over 85 clients. I am an advocate for seniors and boomers as we forge through this life stage, this river of aging. I hear amazing stories. I hear family histories, jokes and some tall tales. I hear family secrets, sometimes shocking in content. Tears are shed as we share the details of life's flow. We cry for those lost to us and for those we will soon lose. I listen. I listen as family members share their frustration, their worries, their anger, and their love as they deal with a way to get help for themselves and their loved ones.

We continue celebrating birthdays with cake, flowers, and a sense of amazement when we note the milestone years. There continues to be room for joy, incredible amounts of joy, despite the setbacks of aging. Making those transitions affirmative is what I want to share with you.

As the owner of *There For You*, I have found some solutions to the issues we all might face in the future. My goal is to share what I've learned and spare you the frustration not only of dealing with your own aging body, but with the issues you could face with your parents.

A little insight now will help you maintain a higher quality of life as you live longer. Boomers are beginning to reassess how they want to spend their retirement years. The magic number to retire won't be 65, as we find ourselves in leaner economic times. We'll need to work longer and make more money to sustain the lifestyle we've created for ourselves. If you're not *retiring* to bed at night, don't even *think* of using the word *retire*! When we do finally stop making our salary our priority, we need to be engaged in life to the point we find new personal frontiers to explore, whether it's in the form of a second career, or in the pursuit of a new diversion or volunteer-oriented position. We had better be in good physical shape to manage it all, too. There is work to be done to make these years powerful and enduring.

Changing Conditions

Recently, I asked a 93-year-old client how old she felt *psychologically*—disregarding her aged body, how old she felt in spirit. She told me she felt like she did when she was 50! That means when I reach the age of 93 and barring any accidents or major illnesses, I'll feel as great as I do now. Meanwhile, the reality that waits can be daunting.

Aging can bring at least some of these conditions for most folks. The changes are usually gradual—good thing, right? Everyone is different. Genetics will play a role, and so will your lifestyle. You can slow some changes by living a healthier lifestyle.

Dexterity is more limited, reaction time is slower, and tasks take longer. Of course, this may make it risky to continue to drive.

Diminished eyesight makes it harder to get around and increases the risk of fall. I attended a training session for caregivers several years ago and one section covered was the topic of diminished eyesight. We were asked to look through various pairs of glasses that mimicked different kinds of sight impairment. It was shocking to see what various conditions can do to one's sight.

Hearing loss can create alienation in social settings. Some people delay the purchase of hearing aids because of the cost and because they are embarrassed to admit they need them. Sadly, sometimes hearing loss is mistaken for dementia.

Poor balance might make a fall more likely. Even the *fear* of falling, can make a person more susceptible to a fall.

Cognitive function can decrease as we age, though it is not a sign of aging itself. Some memory loss is normal. The risk of dementia rises as we age. There are many types of dementia; Alzheimer's being one type.

Depression is common for many reasons. Loss of friends and sometimes a mate is obviously sobering as are thoughts of our own mortality. Just dealing with the issues of health and mobility can be a cause for depression. Feelings of inadequacy may be acute. Frustration can be high for those who must face an ever-increasing number of losses in their personal lifestyle.

Fears of isolation and insecurity can be strong, particularly if we become dependent on help from others. The loss of independence is one of the hardest conditions to accept for most people.

Diminished appetite can increase to the point of malnutrition if someone isn't monitoring the situation because our sense of taste and smell isn't as sharp. Sometimes there isn't as much enjoyment from eating as there was in younger years.

The bones may become weaker, more fragile and less dense.

The metabolism is slowed and the body thickens, particularly when nothing is done to stay in shape through exercise and healthy eating.

Skin gets thinner and less elastic making it more prone to tears and bruising.

Hair thins all over the body and it is less moisturized.

Organs don't perform with the efficiency we've taken for granted for so many years.

Life is full of cycles. Learning to live with the more unpleasant cycles, symptoms and awkwardness, means we have to find the grace to accept them.

Dementia and Alzheimer's Disease

I find myself emotionally drawn to all my clients, but those who live with dementia have a special place in my heart. To lose oneself through the haze of dementia has to be one of the most frustrating, hopeless feelings a person can experience. These are people still involved in life, though certainly with a different perspective. Depending on the type of dementia suffered, many still feel a need to be useful in their daily lives, until their dementia progresses to a later stage.

When I became involved with clients who had *any* form of dementia, I didn't know what to expect. I wondered if I could help in the way they needed. What would they think of me? How would I relate to them? I was marginally less jittery than Jell-O. I've had to learn to communicate differently with those clients who suffer. Not only do their families and loved ones suffer, but the victims of this disease are oftentimes aware of what their future will be like. Some people respond with deep despair, but I've also been amazed at their capacity for humor. The gamut of emotions is endless.

Now I look forward to visiting some of the memory care units where my clients live. Though I'm certainly not there for the long hours the caregivers work, I have an appreciation for their work. Through the fatigue, the frustration, and the exhaustion that comes with dealing with people who have limited powers of memory, I also see the commitment, the concern, the humor these hard-working people bestow on the residents. I have not dealt with someone who exhibits violent or aggressive behavior, but the caregivers have won my respect as I've watched them deal calmly with those residents. I'm certainly not an authority and can only give you my personal insight, which I am more than happy to do here. Most of the time I spend with clients is great. There are poignant moments, too, and tears, and wise insightful thoughts expressed even through the fog of dementia.

I have learned to live in the moment, and sometimes within the *delusion* of the person I am working with at the time. One client still waits for her husband; Ivy has forgotten her husband died almost 25 years ago. She will say something perfectly lucid, be very involved in our conversation, and then say she is waiting for him to come and get her so she can go home. She tells me they are planning a trip to Europe in the fall. Sometimes she is upset because she thinks he is having an affair with another woman and is going to marry her. When that happens, I tell her she's had a bad dream, but that it is *just* a dream, and that her husband has been gone for a long time. She is relieved and grateful I reminded her! When she is happy and making an offhand remark about him coming for her, I just let her comment pass.

There are many kinds of dementia that present differently. Often, it takes a professional to define a specific kind, and even then, it can still be a guessing game.

Most dementias fall into two categories and have several subtypes within each category as well. Cortical Dementias affect the cerebral cortex area of the brain. This area controls the senses, language and thought processes, along with how we associate those thoughts into experiences that mean something to us. **Alzheimer's Disease** is found in this part of the brain and is one of the most common types of dementia. Another type of dementia in the cortical group is **Dementia with Lewy Bodies**. I had never heard of this one until I had a client who had Parkinson's with Lewy body dementia. People who live with this type tend to have cognition issues that come and go. Sometimes there are hallucinations, too. **Vascular Dementia** is often a result of strokes. Brain function declines and causes memory loss as well as a loss of reasoning skills. Sometimes people develop aphasia, which means they lose the ability to speak or to understand language. There are more types of dementia in the cortical group, but these three are the most common.

The Sub-cortical Dementias are in the second type of dementia. The area of the brain affected here is *below* the cortex. **Huntington's Disease**, often genetic, falls into this group. It affects nerve cells in the brain and causes uncoordinated body movement, emotional upsets, and overall decline in cognitive ability. **Parkinson's Disease** can also cause a type of dementia, particularly in the later stages. Parkinson's causes the body to move sporadically due to the decline in brain cells; too little dopamine is produced. As more nerve and brain cells are affected, more dementia is seen.

Some symptoms of dementia are considerable memory loss, loss of reasoning ability, inappropriate behavior, time and place disorientation, inability to follow direction, neglect of personal upkeep and hygiene, paranoia, loss of communication skills, changes in gait or motor skills, and changes in balance. Of course, other things besides dementia can cause these symptoms; a doctor's evaluation is necessary. Sometimes medications can mimic the symptoms of dementia.

When a diagnosis of dementia is given, it can come as a complete shock. Denial is a common reaction. Huge lifestyle changes must be faced; a new reality looms. Some family members react by arguing with their loved one when they can't recall details, make mistakes, or behave inappropriately. They find themselves embarrassed by the actions and comments of the person who is suffering. Confusion, frustration, and anger reign as everyone reacts to the diagnosis. If any of this hits home for you, get the emotional support and guidance you're going to need from a trained professional as soon as possible and know you're not alone as you face this new dimension of life. As you learn to adapt to your loved one's changing personality, you'll find ways to make those tasks easier to accomplish.

Here are some tips I've learned:

> Change your reality for a moment—you get to play act! If you find Ted or Mary are upset about something that isn't possible, step into their reality for a moment and try to suggest a solution to the problem. Let's say Ted tells you he is waiting for the bus to take him home (and he is actually in the dining room of the secured unit where he has recently moved). Instead of insisting to him that he doesn't live at home anymore and that he is here in the dining room, you might suggest you'll find out when the bus is coming. Maybe you can suggest he sit down and have a cup of coffee while you get the information. One of the nice things about memory loss is that it doesn't take long to redirect

19

the person's thoughts by changing the subject. By the time you get Ted his coffee, you can ask a question about something else and he will have forgotten all about the bus—at least for a while.

Don't argue or try to change their mind. Mary won't understand what's wrong, she could be even more confused, angry, and may retreat further into herself. It isn't possible to make a reasonable suggestion to someone who cannot think with the coherence they once possessed.

Acknowledge their frustration. Mary can't put into words why she is upset, or maybe she gives you another reason for her unhappiness. If you can let her know that you empathize with her feelings by responding with understanding, then you are more likely to redirect her train of thought and introduce another activity. Sometimes, people just want to be heard. They have a need for reassurance that someone understands their plight (whether it is missing the 'bus' or feeling out of sorts because they didn't sleep well).

Be patient. Don't expect quick responses or comments—not going to happen! Maybe they walk in circles because of their confusion, or because they are trying to fathom where you're asking them to go. People with dementia can sometimes have a slow or irregular gait when they walk. It can take longer to put on clothing or to put on a coat for a trip outside.

Wait a few minutes. I have a client who has forgotten how to sit down in a chair—sometimes. If he is confused, rather than trying to herd him to the chair and help guide him into it, I wait and then ask him again a minute later. Sometimes his automatic response kicks in, and he sits down as he always did. If Betty (who hasn't eaten all day) needs to eat more of her dinner but tells you she's not hungry, wait a few minutes and ask again or offer a bite. You may very well get a completely different, more cooperative response.

Keep your voice calm and soothing. Be careful what emotions you let play out on your face and in your voice. Nuances are picked up and can help or hinder. You may be worried about something else that has nothing to do with the present situation, but your loved one could interpret that frown to mean you're upset with them. I remember one woman who reached into her pocket and then handed me her dentures! I thought, "Ick!" I smiled at her and said thank you....

Try to create positive feelings and situations. We all need a friend. Be there. Find joy in simple activities. Sometimes just sitting together to enjoy the warmth of the sun coming through a window can be soothing. Look at a magazine together. Find a quiet corner to sit in, or take a walk. Visit a good neighbor. Create a bouquet of flowers, or plant some bulbs in the garden. Pet an animal. Color a picture. Toss a ball together—it's good for hand and eye coordination, too!

Include others. I've found that by talking with someone else or *about* someone else in the room, my client has something else to focus on besides his or her troubles and in a few minutes, they've forgotten all about the issue. Again, his or her short-term memory can work to everyone's advantage.

Use short sentences. If you need to give or ask directions of your loved one, use short, direct sentences as they will be understood better. Speak a little more slowly and look directly at the person you're addressing.

Find the humor. When something embarrassing happens, whether it's an accident when someone doesn't make it to the bathroom, or a spilled drink, make light of it. Talk about how you've done the same thing and find the humor in what's happened. Be silly. If Ted doesn't want to take his medicine, act silly and try to humor him into taking it.

Tell a joke. I usually recite a few jokes repeatedly. It's another way to distract someone when you need to and, again, it helps those who have short-term memory. Maybe I have short-term memory, too, since I can usually only remember a couple jokes!

Show your support. Don't forget the value of a hug, or the holding of a hand. We all need touch; it's been my observation that people who suffer from dementia may also feel insecure; they need touch more than most.

Tell them how much you love them. Who doesn't need that reassurance—no matter how much is going wrong at that moment, we are still lovable and worthy of love.

Treat them with as much dignity as you show to others. Even if their words and sentences don't make any sense, give them the opportunity to try to finish speaking. If they look like they believe they've communicated what they were trying to say, nod in agreement as though what they said was all perfectly logical and natural. Again, don't react strongly to mistakes or accidents. By helping them maintain their dignity, they feel better about the situation.

Brighter lighting. Sometimes bringing more light into the room or area can decrease shadows and therefore decrease the incidences of hallucinations for those who suffer from them.

One thing struck me to the core when I first started working with my dementia clients in the memory care units where they lived. We take our freedom for granted in the United States. We believe it is a right for each one of us. These people have lost that right, and what a profound loss it is for them. I don't think that loss should ever be taken lightly. Considerable evaluation and thought should be given before anyone is placed in a unit where they will not be allowed to leave under their own volition. I have experienced instances when I've felt a decision to place someone in a secured unit was for the convenience or advantage of the staff, and not necessarily because it was the best solution for the resident. This should never happen. Only when someone needs to be admitted for his or her own protection and oversight should such a solution take place.

People can suffer with dementia and don't necessarily need to live in a memory care environment. It depends on what type of dementia they have, the progression rate of the dementia, what family support is available, and what resources they have to tap. If someone with Alzheimer's is living in his or her own home, you should know the disease *will* progress. At some point, family caregivers will probably not be able to continue care for their loved one and will be forced to find another home for them where they will be safe and cared for by an experienced staff.

More tips:

If you are one of those caregivers, I would urge you NEVER to tell a loved one you promise not to put them into a "home." You don't know what situation you'll find yourselves in at some point and it may be the ONLY solution. Promise instead, to make the most loving, careful decision you can for them with their best interest in mind.

Reach out; when someone asks if you need help, say YES! I've watched the caregiver become worn down to a point he or she is in worse shape than the person with dementia. Many service organizations, churches, and local or state organizations can offer guidance and help. Some employers are beginning to recognize the need for support of family caregivers, as well. There is an amazing amount of information online and there is local support for families that are suffering.

Many institutions offer adult day care for your loved one. Take advantage of it so you can recoup and revive yourself in order to continue giving the excellent care you are giving at home. Activities are planned, field trips are taken, meals and snacks provided, and opportunities to make friends abound, all as part of the program.

Find out what in-home care is available to assist with showers and meal preparation and companionship if you find yourself unable to do it or if you need a break.

23

Take advantage of volunteers who can come in for a couple hours while you run errands or go to lunch with a friend.

Keep in touch with family and friends—for your benefit as well as your loved one's benefit.

Don't let your own health suffer from lack of attention. Caregivers are at a much higher risk of health-related illnesses than someone who is not a caregiver.

By the way, most family caregivers are women, even when it means taking time off work to provide that care. Though there are male caregivers, too, women provide 50% more of their time for caregiving than men do. No matter what your case, find support.

Dancing with Rose is a non-fiction work by Lauren Kessler that will give you a peek into the world of caregiving. The author worked for several months in a secured memory–care unit for adults who suffered with memory loss. Lauren worked there to get first-hand experience with the intention of writing about it. I found her book to be honest, spot on, and humbling.

Still Alice by Lisa Genova will give you a different perspective. When you read her book, you'll feel like you've experienced first-hand what it must feel like to have Alzheimer's disease. Her insightful, realistic novel is a must-read for anyone who knows someone with Alzheimer's. In this fictional work, Alice, a Harvard psychologist who is at the height of her career, slowly begins to realize something is very wrong. She finds herself forgetting things that shouldn't be forgotten. She hasn't just forgotten where she put her keys. One afternoon she can't remember how to get home after going for a walk. She's lived there for years. You can feel the denial, the dread, the despair, when Alice realizes what is happening to her mind—what is happening to the very essence of who she is as a person. The shock to her family is palpable.

I continue to read several companies are on the cusp of finding a cure for Alzheimer's and slowing some other dementias. Support those companies and their research—help can't come soon enough.

Plan Ahead

The phone rings and I find myself engaged in a conversation with a fellow boomer who is grappling with decisions about the care of aging parents. I hear things like, "Mom gets confused taking her medicine now." Or, "We were out of town for a couple days and Dad reassured us he would be okay. He wasn't; Dad fell. He laid there for 20 hours because he couldn't get up or get to the phone." Or, "My sister and I live out-of-state and Mom needs to go to the doctor to have her blood pressure checked periodically. We can't take her as often as she needs to go."

As adults, we all like to live independently with all the freedom to do as we please. Shock alert: so do our parents! It's hard to imagine that the independent lifestyle we all know won't last forever. Of course, life has a funny way of dropping a few surprises right in one's lap. Too many times, a crisis forces family members and friends to make hasty decisions. Sometimes it's a fall with broken bones. Sometimes it's because the caregiver is not able to do everything for their loved one anymore. Maybe a stroke or heart attack or a bout with cancer has forced a change. Such a major transition can be daunting. Problems arise when plans for a lifestyle change are put off too long. The aftermath of such a *rushed* change is often reflected in hurt feelings, disappointment, disillusionment, depression, denial, and anger.

Thelma lived alone at 90 and was completely independent. Her mind was good and she was still physically active and alert. She was involved in her community and had a great social life. Two months ago, she had a stroke. Her children swooped in while she was in the hospital, sold her home and all that was in it and moved her to a care community. They didn't discuss any decisions with their mother, the recipient of all these life-altering results. The children went back to their routine leaving Thelma reeling. She was angry and in shock. She suffered mentally and physically and two months later, was not the same confident woman. Her stroke is not to blame for <u>all</u> her changes. Don't let this happen to your loved one. Seek guidance from a senior care manager who can work with everyone in the family.

If you plan, and do your homework, you may find the transition easier for you and for your family. Set some goals—both short-term and long-term goals. Decide what type of lifestyle is desirable and affordable. The good news is there are many options today and the goal is to maintain everyone's independence for as long as possible.

A year ago, I had a chance encounter with a woman about my age. She was saying goodbye to her mother who was living in the memory unit of a local retirement community. I had seen the daughter a few times when she was there to visit. Though we hadn't spoken, we'd exchanged smiles and waves. On this particular afternoon, I caught her in a vulnerable moment and she shared with me how difficult her family's life had become. Her father had suffered a stroke. Her mother was showing signs of early stage Alzheimer's. Until her father had his stroke, he had been her mother's caregiver. When he had to go to a rehabilitation center, their world was turned upside down. The entire family was affected with no time to consider the consequences of such a huge life change.

Her mother was in a constant state of anxiety and was hard to appease because she couldn't remember her husband wasn't at their home. She just knew he was coming to get her any minute. Her mother had asked me several times to take her home, *please*. She didn't understand why she was "locked-up." She pleaded with anyone who would listen, asking for help to call home.

Her daughter had a long commute to visit and had a busy family life of her own. One of her daughters had her own serious health issues. She was torn as she tried to juggle everything. She wanted to appease her mother's anxiety and found herself trying to visit as often as she could while keeping her own family happy. She was getting lost in the shuffle and didn't have a minute for herself.

When her father was finally released from rehabilitation, it was determined he was still not strong enough to return home; he took a room in the same community as his wife, though not in the memory wing. He struggled to adjust but it wasn't going well. He was angry with his children for "putting them in a home," for "not caring about them," and "for just wanting to forget about them and lock them away." Her father was explosive and irritated and her mother was even more confused. I felt the daughter's pain as I saw her tears and the anguish in her face while she relayed her story.

I later witnessed another frustrated child of this same couple. He was trying to explain to his parents that he needed to get back to work and that he didn't have time to argue with them. He was concerned about the effect all his absences would have on his job. My heart went out to all of them.

Does any of this sound familiar? I think we've heard some version of this scenario and it is heart wrenching. What do you do as you watch your parents grow older and become more vulnerable? I don't think any of us is ready for the decline that will eventually come to us. Depending on your own family dynamics, it can be a difficult time as everyone wades through the decision-making process that waits. Sensitivity should be the order of the day.

Issues

The Big Talk

I told you in the last chapter about the woman who was dealing with her parent's struggle after her father had a stroke. Her mother was living with the beginning stages of Alzheimer's.

The personality traits each family member wields can be interesting, to say the least. Some families who communicate well don't have too many issues. Good for them. Often times, there is at least one sibling who chooses not to be involved or who can't be involved because they live too far to commute. There are still ways they can help. Perhaps they can manage or oversee the paperwork or healthcare issues, even if not the physical care. I see both situations and variations of them with my clients.

When I took a trip last year to visit *my* mom and dad, I suggested to my siblings we have a family meeting for The Big Talk. I was a little nervous. I'm the oldest, and because I come face-to-face with the issue so often, I decided I should be the one to spearhead the topic. Gulp.

Most fortunately, for our family, it went very well. In fact, our parents were relieved we had brought up the subject. Daddy said he was glad we finally realized they were not going to live forever! They proceeded to tell us what type of care they envisioned for themselves. They clued us in on their financial picture and shared lots of other information, too. They told us where to look for insurance policies and paperwork. We discussed their will. They have already made funeral arrangements and paid for them. I think we all felt a real sense of accomplishment and satisfaction after the meeting. The wee bit of Southern Comfort we consumed didn't hurt, either!

I started the conversation by telling them the story I told you regarding the daughter dealing with her parents. I then told them, "I needed," and "we needed." Do you know many parents that don't respond to something their children *need*? I think our parents continue to *parent* all their lives; therefore, they open themselves up give you what you need. *Voilà!* The conversation begins...

Find an opportunity for some quiet time or a time when the original family unit *is* together. In our case, everyone was gathered during the weekend for a family wedding. I think asking questions about your parent's wishes and desires will get things started with the right tone. Remember, this whole thing just starts the dialogue; you're not trying to make decisions. It will take many discussions and lots of time probably.

This isn't about you. Later in the conversation, I think it is appropriate to discuss the effect their decisions could have on each member of the family. For example, some siblings might be caring for their own grandchildren, or still working full-time. If their help were required, how much lead-time would they need to take a parent to a doctor's visit? Would the parent(s) consider moving out of state to be in closer proximity to their children? What kind of impact would that have on everyone's life, including their social life? What expectations would everyone have?

Listen hard to everyone's comments, especially your parent's concerns and desires. Ask your parents what worries them. Sincerely listen and pay attention to their nonverbal cues, too. If they feel actively involved in the whole decision-making process, you'll have a better conversation. Let them know how much you respect them. It may be a revelation to everyone that if they aren't involved in the decisions being made, *someone else* will make those decisions *for* them should a crisis arise. It may not be what they had in mind at all!

I also brought up the issue of driving. Though my parents are both still capable drivers, we talked about the time when they would need to turn that responsibility over to someone else. Of course, because this is one of the last hurrahs of independence, it is a tough hurdle for most people. I found approaching the subject with a little humor goes a long way. On my web browser, I typed in the words "how to talk to your aging parents about their future." There is lots of information out there. See what suggestions you can pick up.

Now that you've thought about your approach with your own parents, save your children the trouble and develop a strategy for your own game plan. Write it down so everyone is in the loop.

Good luck, and know I'm right there with you!

Time to Turn in the Car Keys

I had a client for a couple years that was truly an old-world gentleman. I miss him, even now. I remember when his daughter first called and asked if I would be willing to visit with her dad once a week. She wanted me to take him out to lunch, to go on outings and take him for a drive wherever he wanted to go in the metro area. He would navigate, and I explored areas that were new to me. She asked that I take him grocery shopping or shop for him. She wanted me to be an extra pair of eyes and ears for the family.

She explained he was having a hard time adjusting to life without driving. He couldn't understand why all his kids were sabotaging his effort to continue driving. After all, Hank lamented, he had been a wonderful driver with a perfect record and there was just *no* reason for their attitude. He said they had taken his car away from him - they had stolen it from him! He was indignant.

In all the time I knew Hank, there was rarely a week that went by without him asking me to please call the Department of Motor Vehicles (DMV) and plead his case. He wanted me to take him down for a driving test. He asked that I call his doctor's office to see if he would approve his ability to drive.

Of course, I couldn't do any of this. Hank was *not* capable of driving anymore. He had suffered a couple strokes. His memory had been impaired, particularly his short-term memory. His reaction time was slow, and his judgment was often spotty. He forgot he had given his car to one of his grandchildren. It had not been stolen at all. His doctor and the DMV were well aware of his story as they heard from him often. His children felt tormented and frustrated. His daughter told me they *had* taken him for driving and written tests on several occasions and he had failed miserably.

34

I was able to help him retain some of his independence by letting him decide when and where we would go. When he brought up the subject, I was able to redirect the conversation most of the time; at other times, I just listened to his frustration and empathized with him. Most of the time, that is all it took; Hank just needed someone to listen. If you are facing a similar situation with one of your parents, you may find articles online that can help.

Of course, not every driver goes kicking and screaming when they're told they need to hand over the car keys. Some instinctively know it's time; they are more insecure in their driving and have already started limiting the distance in which they're willing to drive. They begin to isolate themselves. There is a reluctance to drive after dark.

Think of your own driving capabilities. Whether it is an aging parent or yourself, evaluate the skills needed to drive. Not safe on the road anymore? Step away from the car...

We **all** take driving for granted. After all, we've been doing it most of our lives. We can hop in the car and go to the store for a quart of milk, we can run over to visit a friend who lives on the other side of town, and we run our errands to the bank and the dry-cleaners. We haul grandkids and visit family, take a car trip out of state. We're independent and dependable. Our psyche is not very adept at accepting the loss of the privilege to drive—and it is a privilege. Remember when you told your 16-year-old exactly that?

Plan ahead and be proactive. No one wants to be responsible for hurting someone. Who wants to live with that kind of nightmare for the rest of their life? One can still remain independent and run your errands with someone else behind the wheel. Think ahead and organize the week a little more. With some advance notice, there are other options available.

Maybe a family member can pick up a few things at the store if just a couple things are needed. Perhaps a neighbor would be willing to take an extra passenger; a little gas money offered would make it more equitable, too.

Some cities have great public transportation. Take a field trip sometime just for fun and note the businesses and services along the route that could be useful someday.

There are private hire transportation companies, too, though it will certainly cost more. Taxi service is available for those times when other options aren't possible. There is even such thing as a pre–paid taxi card making it easier as no one is scrambling for cash. Selling the car could provide funds to pay for transportation expenses.

Many times adult care agencies can take their clients where they need to go. Check first, to see what they are able to do and whether they have a minimum number of hours required for their services. Find out how much advance notice they need.

The National Center on Senior Transportation (NCST) has great information on its website to inform you about finding transportation options in your area. As a boomer who still has a few years to drive (hopefully) I am pinning my bets on a car that can drive itself. I'll sit back with the newspaper and my coffee and wait for "Jeeves" the car to get me there!

Aging in Place

"Aging in place" is a catchphrase that has caught fire with boomers who are dealing not only with their aging parents but with the reality that they, too, will turn the same corner sooner rather than later.

When asked, almost everyone tells me their wish is to continue living where they are right now. Though usually in the family home, it could also mean the retirement community in which they live. Cost continues to increase in adult retirement buildings. By the time boomers decide where they want to spend their retirement years, there could be a shortage of retirement places with so many boomers hitting the market at once. Most people cannot sustain the monthly payments of $3,000 to $6,000 for any length of time, if at all. More people will have no choice but to stay in their homes and rely on family for help when the need arises. Past generations did exactly that, and we are seeing a resurgence of that trend. Family members make up the highest percentage of caregivers in the home. Sometimes it works; sometimes it doesn't. Emotions among family members can run high and be volatile. If you're a caregiver for a family member, get the support you need and don't feel guilty about it.

It's time to put some thought into what aging in place means. Staying in the family home presents its own issues. Everything is great until a health related concern arises. Maybe the stairs are too much of a challenge lately. Maybe it takes too much effort to do the yard work or keep the house clean. It could be easier to stay home rather than drive to the social events of the past. It isn't uncommon for families to be in denial that someone is having a little trouble. None of us wants to admit we can't do all the things we used to handle with little care. Sometimes it takes an outsider—a mediator—or a professional senior care manager to put things in perspective in an objective way. It might be easier on everyone to remove family members from the uncomfortable position of making decisions for other adults in the family. A professional will have resources to tap into and can save some legwork, too.

It can be *huge* to have needed help with the cleaning and yard work, help with shopping and errands, transportation, or even having someone there who can provide companionship when other family members are not available. For those with diminishing ability performing their activities of daily living (ADL's), such as dressing, bathing, and toileting, and eating, help is readily available. It can be advantageous to hire help through a home health company, a home care company, or with a reputable private caregiver. You don't have to know exactly what you need before you call. Often times someone will come to your home for a free consultation. You're not required to "sign up" when they visit to do an assessment. They can make suggestions based on what your situation is and what future requirements you anticipate.

Home care companies can provide:

Non-medical care by running errands, doing light housekeeping, fixing meals, providing companionship and transportation.

Personal care involving those ADL's I mentioned. Fall risk is common with some health issues and if someone is there to assist, the risk is certainly much less.

Home health companies can provide:

Medical care as they have skilled nurses or professionals that have been trained in basic medical care. If wound care is needed, injections or blood draws required, these are the folks for you!

Hospice care can be another option for terminally ill people provided by a home health agency or as a stand-alone option. Some people think hospice is only available in a skilled setting. This is not true. These companies can help with the transitions made providing hands on help, as well as emotional and medical support. Most people don't realize they also offer many ancillary services such as massage, aromatherapy, music therapy,

acupuncture and acupressure for instance. They offer emotional support for everyone involved, not just the patient.

When you enlist the help of an agency, the agency provides the caregiver
and manages those employees. They should screen their employees by
doing background checks, etc., as well as provide training for them. Ask
to get details. I would also be sure they are licensed, bonded, and insured
to protect the family using their services. Working with an agency that has
several employees can be advantageous; if one caregiver isn't a good
match or is ill, there will be others who can take over.

Hiring a private caregiver has its advantages, too. You'll want to find
someone with a good reputation in the community. Ask doctors and their
staff, a social worker who works with seniors, a guardian who serves seniors; ask people you trust. Adult community centers might have a few
names for you as well. Your loved one may be happier interacting with
just one person and can develop a real friendship that has beneficial effects for all parties. Without agency fees, it may be less expensive.

Making these changes can be gradual. Other help can be hired in the
future as needs become apparent. Hiring a housekeeper or lawn person
would be a way to start the process. Hiring a daily money manager is a
wonderful way to offload the hours of work dedicated to keeping up with
bill–payment, paperwork, or overseeing all of the mail. It can be hard to
keep up as arthritis makes writing difficult, as eyesight presents limitations, or memory issues become a problem for some. Using a daily money manager while you're on an extended trip is a great way to experience
the process. Not everyone wants their children to be privy to their financ-
es and not every adult child wants the responsibility or has the time.

Consider remodeling your home *now* to accommodate any possible mobility limitations in the future. Incorporating *universal design* concepts in the
home where you intend to stay is a way to be proactive. Many technolog-
ical innovations are available today. More are coming in the near future
offering positive solutions for all of us. I find that reassuring and I intend to
take advantage of as many as possible.

More about Universal Design

Universal design is a concept that applies to many areas of life, but we are specifically talking about buildings and homes in this instance. Structures are built or modified with features that are suited to *everyone*—no matter what their age or ability. I would urge all designers, contractors and builders to consider the concept when working on all of their projects. Just as people have become more aware of ways to preserve Earth's resources, and communities are creating sustainable environments, my hope is we will become more educated about designing places and spaces for everyone. It isn't always about aging. It isn't always more expensive, either. It is as difficult for a mother trying to negotiate the steps from the garage into the house with a toddler and a couple bags of groceries as it is for someone with a walker or wheelchair.

With universal design, one can remain where they chose to live for as long as they wish—*regardless* of their abilities or disabilities. Several websites have information regarding this *lifetime living* concept. Depending on what changes are incorporated, it could very well be less expensive to remodel with a **one-time** cost rather than spending the same amount or more **each** year in an adult retirement community. If you are already exploring building or remodeling options, look for businesses or companies that have a CAPS designation. CAPS stands for Certified Aging-In-Place Specialist. These go-to folks can help you tailor your needs to your specific budget.

Cabinets can be lowered and varied, doorways widened, appliances reconfigured, stairs eliminated or modified with the addition of a lift. Ramps and handrails can be installed, bathrooms and kitchens modified, grab bars that are integrated into the design can be added - just to name a few. You would find it difficult to detect these added features because they can be added seamlessly into the design of the space. Of course, all of this refers to the *physical* dwelling.

Technologically, there are several devices out there to make life easier, too. Several personal emergency response systems (PERS) are available to alert caregivers when someone needs help. Some are worn as a pendant around the neck; some are worn on the wrist. Some models require the owner to push a button when help is needed. The newest technology does not rely on the individual to "sound the alarm." These systems can tell the difference between a person lying down and an actual fall and will respond accordingly to the person or entity designated when the system was installed.

Smart monitors learn a person's natural movements around their home and yard and can detect a change in pattern. If something is amiss, an alert is sent to the designated caregiver. Let's say Vanessa gets up at 7:30 every morning, gets her coffee and steps outside to pick up the paper. The system is aware of her normal patterns. If Vanessa doesn't get up around her usual time in the morning, a call is made and someone is alerted so help can be sent her way if necessary. For example, her son might call her and discover she's just having a lazy morning. Some systems even have GPS through specified cell phones that track a senior with a busy lifestyle.

Automated medication dispensers can be preloaded with medications by someone responsible. When it's time for a dose, the appropriate drawer or compartment opens and an alert is given to remind someone to take his or her medication. If the recipient forgets a dose, a call is placed to that individual first. If there is no response, then more calls are placed down the line until the issue is resolved and the medication has been taken.

Simplified cell phones are also a big hit with seniors with fewer bells and whistles and larger keypads, making the phone easier to use.

All of these devices have a monthly monitoring fee in addition to the cost of the device itself, but it would be interesting to compare the cost differences between the total monthly fees and the monthly rent and care points at an assisted living community.

There are user-friendly computers or monitors that make it easy for loved ones to stay in touch—even if there is limited computer experience. A computer that allows the user to access email, view photos, and get on the internet would probably be enough for many users. I would also be sure there was good security to protect the system against spam and any viruses or malware.

Did you know there is even a toilet seat that can be installed on any toilet that will make a trip to the bathroom easier? The seat fits a standard toilet, although there needs to be an electrical outlet installed behind the toilet itself. The seats have a bidet-like spray of water (and a dryer on some models) that facilitate cleanup. One's dignity and privacy can be preserved and the need for assistance can be reduced or eliminated while hygiene is heightened. Installing one of these on a raised toilet would make life even easier.

Did any of you see in the news that Google has been working to perfect vehicles that can drive themselves? We won't have to drive ourselves or commandeer a driver when we become risky behind the wheel. Google is currently working on a project where the vehicle drives itself using artificial intelligence software. According to the article I read, they've already clocked 1,000 miles without a driver though there was someone on board who could take over if something went wrong. They've totaled 140,000 miles with only a little human control.

We won't see these cars in the showroom any time soon, but I have great hopes we'll see it in our lifetime. I read somewhere recently; the day may come when it is illegal for anyone to sit in the driver's seat of a car! I suspect that *won't* happen in our lifetime.

All this technology is reassuring and makes me feel hopeful for the future. Start Googling all this stuff; you'll be amazed. Refer to the Helpful Links at the back of the book. Now if we can just solve some of the biggies like a cure for Alzheimer's and Parkinson's, and cancer. We won't live forever, but while we're here, the quantity and quality of our lives will be enhanced.

Sometimes a Move Makes More Sense

Some people opt for a retirement community for adults 55 and older. In choosing a community, you'll want to consider what options are available should your needs change and more help is required. It's a great idea to check around and find a community that serves your needs. There are several options from independent living to assisted living, residential care, or skilled nursing. Adult care homes are another option. People prohibited from being on their own due to memory loss can benefit from adult day care (also called adult day services). This gives their regular caregiver a break. All kinds of information about each type of lifestyle can be found on the web, but here is a brief description of each. Campuses that offer a continuum of care will offer choices that see their residents through most stages of health during the course of their life. Remember, too, if choosing to live in a retirement building, a second person living in the rented space increases the monthly cost significantly.

An independent living community has apartments or small cottages that offer no personal care, but offer meals and housekeeping and some transportation options to its residents. There are more involved activities and social options. Independent living may or may not incorporate universal design in their units. Assisted living buildings can offer anything from a small studio to a larger two-bedroom apartment. Residents generally receive three meals a day, housekeeping, and assistance with ADLs (activities of daily living) as well as some transportation options. The more help one needs, the higher the cost. A typical assisted living apartment includes a kitchenette with a small sink, refrigerator and a microwave. There is also a private wheelchair–accessible bathroom with a shower. Residential care buildings offer many of the same features as an assisted living building, but rooms and bathrooms may be shared or private. Skilled nursing is continued, round-the-clock care. This option can be the most cost prohibitive, but sometimes necessary, depending on the needs of the individual. The setting may resemble a more hospital-like setting, though some modern buildings try to make the rooms as warm and inviting as possible. There is professional staff in attendance round the clock. Skilled nursing is also appropriate for rehabilitation after hospitalization. Residents can receive different therapies there. All of these options offer some form of social activities to the residents. The more independent you are, the more activities are offered. In my opinion, the options offered could be more creative, but that is another subject. *Adult care* <u>homes</u>, or <u>foster care homes</u>, are privately owned homes that have been renovated to offer a bedroom and sometimes a private bathroom from four to six people with onsite care by the owners and usually one or two paid staff members. These homes are less expensive than a commercial care setting. Social activities are usually more limited. Because there are fewer residents, they can offer more personal care around the clock and they create more of a home environment. <u>Adult day care</u> (or <u>adult day services</u>), is an option that provides anywhere from 10 to 12 hours of supervised care and activities, includes meals, and even outings. Licensing varies from state to state, and from type of care being offered in different retirement communities.

Another option coming into vogue now is sometimes referred to as the "granny pad." There are some innovative companies manufacturing small modular homes that can be dropped on the property of a family member. These are small, self-contained apartments or cottages. They offer an independent lifestyle that has the advantage of having assistance a few steps away. Many city and county codes are changing to allow such options as long as they are being used for the intended purpose of helping a family member with limited capability. I think this option will become more popular.

If a move to retirement living is the answer, how big a place do you want and at what cost? What do you do with a lifetime's worth of accumulations, family pictures and mementos? Everything has to be considered and much downsizing is necessary. Who gets what? How can things be divided fairly among siblings? What are the things you most want to take with you?

There is the turmoil of deciding just *how* you're going to facilitate the move. How much will it cost to move everything? What kind of help can you elicit from friends and family? Are they even *in* a position to help? Do you worry about burdening them? If money permits, it may be easier for everyone if a moving service is involved for some of the packing and moving decisions.

Start planning now—there couldn't be a better time. If you're the child of an aging parent, bring up the subject by asking if any plans have been made should something happen. If you're the aging parent, do your kids a favor and make some of these decisions. Everyone will have a different answer for what matters most to them.

Take a deep breath. You'll figure this all out. Many resources will help you get there.

Helping your Parents Get Ready for a Move

If staying in their own home is not a possibility, then your parents are going to need to downsize and organize for a move. Ideally, take several months to facilitate the move. As I've said, too often it is a crisis that gets everyone in a panic and that's when regrets can occur. If your parents cringe and are overwhelmed even *thinking* about the big job in front of them, you might consider the possibility of hired help. Several companies specialize in moving seniors. It can be expensive but can bring such a smooth transition that it's worth the cost to some people. Look for a senior move management company that belongs to the National Association of Senior Move Managers (NASMM). Not only will you find companies that know what they are doing, they are also bound by ethical, trustworthy practices. You can relax knowing your parents are with reliable people. Let me give you an example. Let's say somebody hides money or other valuables in little nooks and crannies around the house—maybe something is tucked inside a book or hidden in the furniture. The move managers with the NASMM designation are familiar with just such tendencies to hide things and are trained to look for them and return them to family. If no one in the family wants what's found, sell those items and help offset the cost of the move managers.

Consider an estate sale, too. Interview at least two estate sale companies; compare their contracts and pricing and ask for references. Get recommendations from happy clients. You need to be cautious about contracts stating the estate sale company becomes the owner of all items as soon when the sale begins. There have been instances where the company prices your things high; then when your things don't sell, they take them and resell them elsewhere. If you had changed your mind about selling a particular item, or wanted to give a neighbor something, you wouldn't have that option anymore.

The estate sale dealer usually gets a flat rate of 30% to 40% of the total sales. If it is a large sale, they may just take 25%. If the sale is small, they may take a larger percentage. If you are expecting them to clean up after the sale, you need to find out if there is a cleanout fee.

If the move is going to be a family effort and everyone is going to pitch in, it will take more time to get it done. Remember this is a very emotional time for everyone. Family dynamics create tense moments. Sorting through and letting go of things owned for a lifetime can be sad and hard to do. How are things going to be divided amongst the family? If an item holds too many memories, maybe it should be kept, even if it means renting a storage unit for a short time so your loved one can get acclimated to his or her new surroundings.

Many people feel they are losing control or losing their independence. After a time, once their perspective has changed and their sense of well-being is restored, they might be able to let go of those possessions. With so many things going out the door, it can be overwhelming. Another option would be to take a picture of that special item to be viewed later. Knowing family members now have it in their possession and safekeeping and that it can be seen again during a visit, might ease the pain of parting with it.

I remember helping a client pack up boxes in her apartment for a move to a different, smaller room in a retirement place. She sat there and cried as I helped her sort items that still needed to be packed. She was reliving memories and having such a hard time. She had more than would possibly fit into her new place. My heart went out to her. She didn't have family there to help. I tried to be very sensitive and caring as we worked out the details. I did hear later that she had made the adjustment and was quite happy with her move. You'll be relieved to know that's usually the case.

To get started, take one room at a time, preferably the smallest. That way, the task won't seem as daunting.

Think about where everything will fit in the new space and how often it will be used. Family china, dish sets, and crystal were more popular with our parents and even with we boomers than they are with the younger generation. If your mom hesitates over letting it go, suggest taking a few pictures, save a teacup and saucer and let the rest go. If a grandchild isn't interested, maybe donating it to a tearoom or a favorite charity would offer a more satisfying solution. If you wish to sell it, be aware decreased demand has lowered prices.

Has the item being considered been used in the past year? If not, it probably won't be in the next year. Limited closet space usually doesn't accommodate many clothes. Think about letting it go.

Some people think if they get rid of something, they'll find they need it later. A reminder that most items can be borrowed or purchased again might help ease the concern.

If you're considering what furniture to take, keep in mind the space where it's going. Draw a floor plan. Tape the outlines in the new place; the people moving the furniture won't have to wait for you to show them. Think about repurposing a piece of furniture. Maybe what was the buffet in the dining room can now be a dresser in the bedroom, particularly if a whole bedroom suite won't fit into the new space. Maybe that same buffet can go into a second bedroom commandeered to be office space and be filled with computer equipment or office supplies.

Most people have several framed pictures, usually on the walls, on tables and shelves. Putting them into one digital photo frame can be a great way to display them—one frame vs. several. Granted, it will take time to scan them and save them, maybe someone who is savvy with a project like that can help.

Finally, once the move is complete and there's time to catch one's breath, many people feel lost, and go through a mourning period. They miss their friends. They miss the freedom they had to come and go as they pleased, and on their own schedule. After some time, they will make the transition. Fortunately, there are many resources available to help ease everyone into the adjustment. Support groups are available at various senior community centers and other locations. Getting involved with those who share a common interest will go a long way in getting settled.

Be patient, sensitive, and supportive as everyone adjusts in the first few months—not just the day or two of the move and the week afterward. It takes time to integrate into this new life change. Take the time to pick up the phone or go for a visit. It can be a wonderful change of pace to take someone out to dinner. Get to know the staff and the administration so you can develop a good working rapport with everyone.

Are You the Caregiver for a Family Member?

I always try to stay on the good side of my adult kids – I remind them of all the good things we did for them and how *amazing* we were as parents! Just in case... Almost everyone will either become a caregiver or receive care from family at some point in their lives. Family members are usually willing to help and have good intentions borne out of love, and concern. Oftentimes, there is even great enthusiasm for being able to help. People commit their time and energy to helping with a warm, loving, and generous attitude.

Sometimes, of course, family relationships are problematic but there is still a need for care. Funds may be short but care is still needed and even reluctant family members might be called into service.

Either way, it is a big commitment to tend to the needs of someone. Even the most enthusiastic caregiver can feel overwhelmed at times. Stress is natural but shouldn't be ignored if it seems to last longer than a couple days. If you're the caregiver, you need to take care of yourself so you'll be able to help. Unpaid family caregivers can suffer emotionally and physically as they continue to give of their time, and their energy.

Take a break. Be sure to include time for to recharge. Listen to some of your favorite music, go read a book, or take a walk. Get away for lunch or dinner with a friend. There is no shame in taking care of yourself. There will be others who can step in to make it possible for you to get some relief.

Don't drop your friends! You need them more than ever. When you need a pressure release, be open with the family and friends in which you can confide. Join a support group for caregivers. It helps to know you're not alone and that others are dealing with the same kinds of issues. You might pick up a few tips for handling different or difficult situations. .

Get to know the nature of your loved one's condition or disease. Talk with the doctor and the medical staff so you're informed about what needs should be met and how to perform them.

Know your limits. Don't be afraid to let everyone know what you can or are willing to do in the way of caregiving. No one person can meet all the needs for another person. We all have our limitations regarding time, effectiveness, and skill.

Be aware of how other family members are interacting with your loved one and with you since your time is more limited. Encourage open communication about what each person is feeling.

It's okay to feel negative, too. Who wouldn't feel negative occasionally when helping someone day after day, hour after hour? If your loved one is living with a chronic condition, knowing your help will be needed for a long time can be hard to accept.

Take advantage of technology that is available today. There are options that could give you more freedom and your loved one more independence.

Please seek information online, at the library, and at agencies and businesses that work in the caregiving field.

Downsizing is to Organizing

<u>Downsize</u> means to economize; rationalize.
<u>Organize</u> means to arrange, to make more effective.

I feel stressed and sometimes *overwhelmed* when there is lots of clutter around the house. I begin to feel life is getting away from me. When everything is in its place and I see lots of space, I feel calmer. I even feel *rejuvenated*. If you are like most people, you have been accumulating for YEARS. It's funny though, I found my mindset changing a few years ago.

My husband and I used to talk about building a larger house. Being what I call a home and hearth person, I love to decorate the house and create beautiful rooms. I've always enjoyed browsing in second hand shops and hunting at garage sales for things that inspire me. Spending time at home gives me a sense of peace and tranquility.

Anymore, it has to be something special for me to buy it. I am beginning to have a sense of satisfaction *letting things go* now! My husband and I have stopped talking about building something bigger.

Now we talk about creating something smaller and on one level where we will certainly incorporate universal design features. Maybe <u>you</u> are considering a smaller house or apartment.

Where to begin…

I always think winter is a good time to reassess what you have. While everything outside is still mostly asleep, there is time to organize by taking a good look at those closets and cupboards and drawers.

Think of it as a time to refresh your surroundings, clean away the clutter, reorganize your things AND your life! After you're finished, maybe there will be time to pursue new hobbies and interests, new opportunities. First a little homework needs to be done.

Even thinking about the process of downsizing can be daunting, much less actually doing the work. This is a time for plotting and organizing to keep everything flowing smoothly. Deciding what to keep, and what to donate (whether it be to family members or your favorite charity) can be overwhelming.

Instead of being overwhelmed by the whole process, break it down into jobs or projects that won't seem so overpowering. There is a lot of information available on many fronts. The internet is invaluable for gleaning information and finding helpful resources.

I've suggested to friends and clients they take a drawer or cupboard each week and organize it. There are 52 weeks in a year. Of course, you'll be too busy around the holidays, but still, that's a lot of space cleared and organized.

Things to consider:

I found this on *Gayle Grace's website, All Things Home*. How many of these questions do you answer "yes" to?

Do you keep:
Piles of magazines because you'll read them someday?
Broken appliances/electronics because you'll get them fixed or hauled someday?
Items someone gave you but you don't really want, but it was a gift, so someday?
Clothes you don't wear because they don't fit anymore but you might get back into someday?
Things you are storing for others (read adult children) because they'll come get them someday?
"Someday is not a day of the week!"

How about those crazy plastic butter containers you've saved all these years—do you really need all 50—oh, and by the way, why is there never a lid that fits? Maybe they're hanging out with all the socks that disappear from the dryer, never to be seen again.

Do you save every pen or pencil that comes into the house? By the time you go through them, most are dried up. Is there still lead in those short little hard-to-grip pencils? Surely, someone can use them! What about all those little half-empty shampoo and lotion bottles collected from hotel stays? Actually, those *can* be donated to a shelter.

Do you have papers saved (and overflowing) in too many drawers and cupboards? Look on the internet for information telling you how long you should keep certain documents and bills after they've been paid. With the rest, you can - Trim the FAT: **You can File it, Act on it, or Toss it.**

> File every day—then it can't pile up. When you bring the mail in, decide immediately what you're going to do with it. Create a mail area and keep a trashcan or recycle bin close. Have a place for the things you're keeping.

> Act by setting up a "to do" file and check if frequently.

> Toss it if it is accessible on the internet; you can look it up when you actually need it. Tossing might be shredding if there is personal information that could get into the wrong hands. If there is too much to shred, many places have shred days open to the community for a nominal fee. If you've clipped articles for others—*give* it to them.

Lots of clothes? I've read we wear 20% of our things 80% of the time. What does that tell you about the rest? Think about whether it fits or if you even *like* it. Comfort has come to mean a lot to me these days, too. If something isn't comfortable, why are you keeping it? I shop second hand and consignment shops for clothes—that way I don't feel guilty donating clothes I've had for too long in the closet. I always find amazing things—some never worn—and I ask myself why I hung on to my old things for so many years.

Now it's time to divide and conquer the rest: Divide things into three categories: To Keep, To Donate, and To Sell.

If you're keeping - organize it all and keep the things you use often in the most prominent, easy to reach places. When I clean up my closet, I organize things by item first, and then by color. You may have a different way of choosing how you organize your closet. A friend has a collection of scarves. She folds some, but also threads others through the links in a five-foot long chain she got from a lighting store. She then hangs the chain from a hook in her closet. She can see all her scarves at a glance. Clever!

If you're *keeping,* don't just put everything in the attic until you can decide later. You *won't*. Make a decision **now**.

If you're donating - determine *when* you're going to donate. Don't forget you can claim a tax deduction. *Ask* (don't tell) your adult children if they are interested in the things you are letting go. Keep in mind they may not be interested so don't force them to take what you have always prized. I'm sure I don't have to tell you there are many organizations and charities that would be happy to take your things if family and friends aren't interested. Just make sure they are clean and in good working order. If not salvageable, get rid of them; no one else will want them either.

Our grown kids think the house is their personal storage unit—forever. Yours, too? Hmm. Set a deadline to pick up anything of yours they've agreed they *do* want, and to take the things they've been storing since they left for college. That should give you a full room, right there!

If you're selling, organize an estate sale or use one of the online sites. Work with a consignment shop. Use the proceeds to go out to dinner or to buy new plants for the yard, or to buy flowers to perk up the room you just organized.

This is how Beth Giles of NW Organizing Solutions spells FREEDOM for us. Though we have some of the same ideas, I think it is good to reiterate.

55

F Focus on goals: What is important to you? Why are you organizing or downsizing?

R Round up: Gather all like items together from all locations.

E Evaluate: Think about each item. Do you use it? Need it? Love it? What is the condition of each thing? Does it fit the space? Quantity: should you add or subtract from the number of items? What type of memories does each item have for you?

E Edit: Parting with your things - Determine what you want to dispose of because they aren't in good condition. Sell items you wish to sell – there are many resources, EBay and Craig's List being two. Give to the community. Could something you have that's in good condition be useful to someone else?

D Decide: Where you're going to store your things?. Think about the location of them, the frequency of use, and the accessibility of each item.

O Organize and contain: Contain your things. Limit the amount of things you have, label the containers, and decide whether you are a person who needs to have open or closed containers to remind you where you've put items. Don't overfill the containers as you may want to add more things later – but don't save too much space or you'll find yourself back where you were with overflowing areas.

M Maintain: Yes, you need to set aside a few minutes each day to put things away and keep things "tuned-up" so you don't have to start over after all your hard work.

Instead of looking at the entire project, Beth says we need to break down the work into small tasks to make it more manageable and less overwhelming.

I have to share another suggestion she has—one with lots of practicality. Most of us have saved <u>every</u> art projects and gift from our children's early years. Beth told us she is one of 10 children. There are now 38 grand-children—all of whom have made their grandmother several gifts over the years. Her mother kept everything and put them in several boxes. Her solution for so many boxes? She took pictures of each item, then had the pictures made into a beautifully bound book for the coffee table. I love it!

Dot your "T's" and Cross your "I's"

You're going to *cross your eyes* when you read this—or at least roll them. Time for a little nitty-gritty on those forms, that paperwork you've been putting off for another day or another year.

I know it won't happen to **you,** but consider what you want family and your doctors to do when it comes to your healthcare interventions. Just for a wild, crazy moment consider the measures and decisions you want hospital staff or your family to make on your behalf should you find yourself in a life–threatening situation. If an emergency arises, or you find yourself on the receiving end of some doctor's scalpel, it would be nice to have all this stuff tied up in one neat bundle. The middle of a crisis is not a good time to make decisions. Those of you who have worked with your parents on these issues already know how important they are to make.

Here's a brief non–lawyerly breakdown of the forms you need to complete. If you have access to a computer, go to The American Bar Association's website and look at all the information available to you. There are so many decisions to consider. If you don't own a computer, go to the library and use one of theirs. A visit with an elder law attorney is always a good idea.

I think most of us realize we should have a <u>will</u> specifying to others how we want our assets and possessions dispersed. Some people choose to have a trust drawn up by their attorney because they have specific needs. If you don't have a will, the state gets to decide how your assets are dispersed. Yikes! I want to make that choice, don't you? You'll need to decide who to appoint executor (your personal representative) and who the beneficiaries are among your esteemed family and friends.

A <u>Power of Attorney</u> is a document that allows another person to act on your behalf should you not be able to manage your legal, business, or financial affairs. A *general* Power of Attorney has broad power to manage your affairs from paying bills to managing household affairs. A *limited*

Power of Attorney does just that—it limits the decisions made by the agent to specific duties spelled out in the document. The Power of Attorney ends when the principal dies (the person that issued the POA).

You will need to complete a living will (or a health care directive). It spells out for your doctor and your family what kind of medical treatments you want should you be unable to state those wishes yourself. Do you want someone else to decide what you need or would you rather make those choices? Give yourself plenty of time to decide what kind of medical treatment you wish to have—or not. Discuss your thoughts with someone you love and trust. Decide which person in your life you can trust the most to carry out your decisions and determinations. Examine your beliefs regarding life support machines, your values and your feelings about diagnostic testing. What heroic measures do you want the doctor to make and for what type of situation? At what point would you want to stop treatment? Be as specific as possible so your desires are clearly understood.

There was a law passed in 1990 that ensures patients are informed of their rights in making decisions related to their health care. If you've ever had a medical procedure at the hospital, you've signed one.

I think it is important to have a POLST form (Physician's Orders for Life Sustaining Treatment) completed and in a prominent place where you live. In an emergency, this form will guide the medical team regarding your wishes for medical intervention while you are still *in your home*. Once you are in the hospital, your living will would come in to play. Not every state has such a form, but many do. Make it a goal to find out and complete one if your state has one.

A durable Power of Attorney for Health Care, also called a health care proxy, should be completed. This lets you appoint *one person* to act on your behalf in a medical situation when you are not able to make decisions yourself. This person, or agent, is responsible for health care decisions only, not financial decisions like a general Power of Attorney. Unlike a living will, which specifies a person's wishes regarding care and treatment, the durable Power of Attorney for Health Care appoints one person who may act at any time for individuals not capable of making medical decisions. They must act in good faith, following the wishes of the person they are empowered to help.

It doesn't hurt to look into the possibility of <u>long-term care insurance</u>. If we plan to work longer and save more, the insurance should help protect those assets from disappearing too quickly as you pay for care. Terms vary in different policies, so you'll need to do a little homework here. Your premiums will be less if you buy it early—while you're in your early to mid–50's. You have to qualify and it will be easier to qualify while you're younger and probably won't have any or many health–related issues. Many people think it will be cheaper to wait until they are closer to a time when they could realistically need it. Not true. Policies offer more options for types of care than they used to; it is hard to *guess* where you might be 30 years down the road!

When you complete an advance directive, you can still change the contents anytime— even at the last minute, if you wish. People tend to think once it is completed, they can never change their mind. Not true. You may revoke any directives you've made or you may change them any number of times.

After you have everything in order, put the forms in a specific place where they can be found if needed. Be sure your doctor, your agent (the person you have asked to carry out your wishes), and an alternate all have a copy. Leave a copy with those family and/or friends you think should be aware of your wishes. For these documents to be valid, you need to be mentally competent at the time the documents are completed.

This book is all about planning the next chapter in our lives, making them positive, productive years. Why not plan the endgame, too?

If you think your family can handle it, have a group session and get everyone organized at once! You could have blank forms ready to pass around, and then get to work. Can you imagine the conversations around the room?

Points for You to Ponder

Occasionally a client will say to me, "Don't get old, it's awful!" I have to chuckle. What does that mean? Am I supposed to die young?

I went to a memorial service recently and was reminded how important it is to live life well, to enjoy life zestfully. The woman who passed away wasn't even a client of mine. She was one of several people I've gotten to know as I spend time with my clients. I've watched her decline, particularly over the past year. When I first met her about three and a half years ago, she was lively, had a cute giggle, and though she couldn't communicate much verbally, even then, she was someone who brought light into the room. She was sweet, and she loved to go to any program in the community where she lived. She would clap, and sometimes call out in response to the person performing, usually in agreement with what they were saying.

As I listened to her family talk about her life, I was again reminded how each one of us is perceived by others in our lives. They talked about what a party-giver she was, how she gardened, traveled, had a beautiful home, had a real sense of fashion, and was someone who appreciated art. She was a go-getter at every age, playing with her children and the family pets. She hiked, she biked; nothing was off limits. Her son chuckled and said she didn't mince words if she thought you were out of line. She had a reputation for telling you exactly what she was thinking!

I want to be remembered with that kind of fondness and humor. I want my family and friends to celebrate my life with appreciation, and a knowledge that I gave it my best, tried to live the way I advocated. That I loved the best I could for each of them, and meant well in all my endeavors. That I followed my heart, tried many things, fed my curiosity about any number of subjects. Just at the end when I draw my last breath, I want to know I lived well, and fully, and that I inspired others to make more of their own lives by my example.

Want to maximize the number of years you live? I need to live for 200 years to get everything I want to accomplish done. I look forward to every day. If my quality of life isn't good because of my health, that's a different story. I am making suggestions here assuming your health will be optimal. Living long and living well have several components. How many times have you heard someone say, "If I knew I was going to live this long, I'd have taken better care of myself?" Now's your chance—do it!

Attitude

Keeping a positive attitude and finding joy in the *ordinary* is important. Having a reason to get up each day with something to look forward to is a key component. I've read you can add 7.5 years to your life just by having a positive attitude.

For people who deal with pain every day and who are limited in their mobility, it is much harder, but I see it happen all the time. I'm always amazed. I hope I could do as well if I were in their shoes. One woman I knew had suffered a major stroke that left her paralyzed on one side. She was confined to a wheelchair and had to have help moving from her bed, to the bathroom, to a dining room chair. She was eager for me to visit each week—not only to chat—but because she wanted me to redecorate the things in her room. She would ask that I move the pictures on the wall, rearrange some of the furniture, or redecorate the tabletops. She still found joy in her surroundings. I know one woman who gets up early so she can look out through a certain window. She loves the way the sun illuminates the landscape. Another man I knew looked forward to a huge bowl of ice cream every day. Even as he neared his last days, he wanted his ice cream!

Posture

Are you sitting up straight as you read this? Correct your posture and remember to STAND-UP STRAIGHT! Like so many of us, I've had trouble with lower back pain, aching shoulders and chronic neck pain. I have sought the help of chiropractors, physical therapists, massage therapists, acupuncturists, and my regular doctor. Though all offered relief, a physical therapist made me really notice my posture. She taught me a couple tricks that made a big difference. If I'm having trouble on a given day, I have that little "ah-ha" moment and I realize I'm not in good form. I realign myself and instantly, the pain is gone. You'll have more air in your lungs, you'll look taller, and you'll look thinner – especially if you get into the habit of holding your stomach muscles tight. Your body's muscles will work more efficiently and you won't be as tired. You want good blood flow with less restriction to the blood vessels and nerves, too. You'll benefit from fewer headaches. You will project confidence and have greater authority. So start today: correct your posture!

Exercise

I'm sure you're tired of hearing about it but here it is—exercise. Your body AND your brain. Yes, I know, but our bodies are made to move—and—exercise is *great* for anti-aging. Your brain needs physical activity in order to keep your cognitive function higher. Resistance training (using weights or your own body's weight) helps build and maintain muscle mass. Exercise helps with balance as you age, especially yoga. If you do fall, you're less likely to break denser bones. Exercise done in mid-life also helps you lead a healthier life when you finally reach those golden years. Find the self-discipline and just do it. Besides, you'll get some of your best thinking done while you work out.

You can add years to your life by lowering your blood pressure, and your cholesterol. You'll increase your sense of well-being, and you'll catch fewer colds and other diseases, especially if you get outside for part of your exercise. You'll improve your overall looks. All your hard work will make you look taller, straighter, and leaner. You'll find your sleep improved. Exercise doesn't prevent all disease, of course. If you *are* in better shape, though, you may allay or at least reduce some of the complications associated with them. Some people diagnosed with diabetes have been able to turn their blood sugar numbers around by adopting a regular exercise program. If you haven't made exercise part of your routine before, walking is a great way to start.

Later, include yoga, Pilates, or other cardio exercise as part of your routine. Join a gym if you would like the support of others. If you're on a budget or want more privacy, do like I do. I rent tapes and DVD's from the local library. If I like them, I go online and buy them. Spend an hour, though! You will still have 23 hours left in your day to get everything else done! Oh I know - you're too busy. You have meetings to attend, phone calls to make, shopping, too many obligations at home and at work.

Here's my challenge to you. Find 15 minutes, five days a week. Just 15 <u>minutes</u>. Do little things: Walk around the room while you're on the phone instead of sitting, park farther away from your destination. Take the stairs. Go pull a few weeds, vacuum a floor, do a few jumping jacks. Walk. If you've never started an exercise program, do yourself a favor. <u>Just do it</u>. Don't quit this time. Make it part of your life. After you've done it for two weeks, add five more minutes. Two weeks later, add another five minutes. Soon, you'll find yourself up to 45 minutes or an hour. Don't be discouraged if you can't find one interrupted hour. It all counts.

We take our health and the ability to walk for granted now, because we can. Too many of my clients struggle *just to walk*. Exercise *now* for the body you'll be living in *later*—it will *thank* you in the future.

Challenging your mind is another form of exercise we need to engage in every day. Doing the daily crossword puzzle is not enough – if it is something you've been doing for years. If it's a new activity for you, then yes, it might offer you a workout. Learning to play an instrument or learning a new language can be very useful. Take a class that interests you. Become involved with new activities and keep up your social life to stimulate your brain. It is a known fact people who are involved with others maintain better brain function. Travel to stimulate your brain as you experience new things. Learn a new dance to exercise your body and your brain. Be curious and read about things that peak your interest. Did you know watching too much television puts your brain in neutral?

Enjoy Eating

If you're not eating a well-balanced diet, you're not doing yourself any favors. While I'm at it, I might as well throw in my two cents regarding portion size. We've been conned into thinking the portion sizes served in restaurants and fast food eateries are correct. A half–cup of cooked rice is a serving, not two or three cups.

If you don't have good eating habits, develop some now and adhere to them. This doesn't mean you can't ever enjoy a piece of chocolate cake; it means you can't do it all the time. If you're not crazy about fruits and veggies, consider preparing them in new, more creative ways. If your meals consist mostly of colorful vegetables and whole fruits and contain a small amount of protein, some dairy, and a few whole grains, you'll do well. Include fiber, and good fats; reduce your sodium. You'll resist illness, have more energy, and recuperate faster when you're ill. Your attitude will be more positive and you'll feel more alert mentally. You'll feel better and your bones will be stronger. I'm not a nutritionist, so don't take my word for it—do the research.

If you've found yourself facing life alone these days, eating dinner at a table set for one can be hard. For dinner, do you find yourself standing at the sink picking at something you found in the refrigerator and calling it good? Do you make a meal of popcorn and diet soda? Do you grab fast food on the way home from work? Pretty much given up grocery shopping? Don't be too quick to give up an important routine that should be satisfying to you on many levels.

Make an event of mealtime. For some, eating alone isn't fun. Consider surrounding yourself with things you enjoy. What about the "good" dishes that sit in the china cabinet most of the year? Bring them out and enjoy the simple pleasure of setting a great table—even with a single place setting. Put a bouquet of flowers on the table. Put on some music to create atmosphere. Some people like to read while they eat. When the weather's nice, eat outside and surround yourself with nature. You *and* the bees can enjoy!

Maybe now is the time to consider having a friend or a grandchild over for dinner. Company can give you the incentive you need to cook something special or fix a favorite dish. Would your grandson or granddaughter benefit from a few practical cooking lessons? This might be an opportunity for quality time (think passing down recipes, techniques and skills). Just think of all the stories you can tell them at suppertime!

Do you have another single friend who would benefit from shared meals? The two of you could plan a couple meals then shop together. Maybe you could meet once a week to cook so you'll have food later in the week.

For a treat to *all* the senses, take advantage of the farmer's markets that abound in your area. You get to meet people, peruse all the fresh, fabulous fruits, vegetables and flowers and other beautiful food. There's usually someone playing music, too. It's very hard not to be caught up in the excitement and the camaraderie between shoppers, vendors, displayed artwork, and even a few furry pooches tagging along. Don't buy more than you can eat in a week!

There are several cookbooks geared toward cooking for one or two people. Check out the library or the internet. When you do make the effort to cook, remember you can make up plates and create your own "TV dinner" to eat later in the week or to put in the freezer.

Why not check out the salad bar at your local grocery store? There are many veggies to choose from, among them, grated carrots, fresh, cut up things like broccoli and cauliflower. You can get what you need without all the prep work. Try roasting vegetables, too. The rich, deep caramelized flavor is divine!

Consult the butcher and have your selected pieces wrapped for one or two servings. Have them wrapped for the freezer just in case you choose to cook them later. Talk to the fishmonger, too. Fish is the ultimate "fast-food." You can usually cook it in 15 minutes or less.

Pick up a rotisserie chicken from your local grocery store and start from there. You can get two or three good meals from one chicken with a little planning. Make chicken enchiladas one night with some of the leftover meat. You might make chicken salad to pile onto a bowl of salad greens or to put in sandwiches. Make a hearty curry soup.

With a little self-determination and research, you'll soon find yourself looking forward to mealtimes again. Good luck and bon appétit!

Become Engaged

Engage is the operative word here. I said earlier that I have so many interests – enough to keep me engaged for more than a lifetime. Find something to channel your mind in another direction—to expand your thinking and increase your knowledge. We haven't lived all these years for nothing. Keep learning—show everyone how lucky they are to know you! Impress your peers and the younger generation. Volunteer; nothing lifts the spirit more and helps you stay involved more than giving and doing for others. As I said earlier, think about your social activities and stay in touch with your friends. Plan activities together.

Make plans for living longer. Visualize it. Save enough money to support your longer life span. Plan how you'll spend your time after you retire from your 9 to 5 job. It won't be satisfying to most people if they aren't involved with something, be it volunteering or pursuing an interest, or by traveling. Get a group of friends together and take a memory maker of a trip. You could start another career. Write a book and enter the world of self–publishing. Learn a new language—then go visit a country that speaks that language. Mentor someone else who would benefit from your years of experience. Teach your grandchildren a special skill that has been unique to you. Get involved with genealogy and become the family historian. Become more adventurous. Enhance your love life—become engaged again. That's another book, right?

More to Share

Travel

What do boomers look for in travel? Not only do we want a more *active* itinerary, we want it to be *interactive* as well.

Our generation isn't content to go on a large bus tour or to sit in deck chairs on a cruise, unless of course, we get to pick the group. We would include our friends and others who share our interests. Walking or biking tours appeal, as do culinary hands-on tours. Smaller, more personal groups within the same age-range are popular. Boomers do not put themselves in the same category as their aging predecessors—most feel and act much younger than their chronological age. As a whole, we embrace a curiosity and willingness to try new things, seek new experiences.

A walking tour at a unique destination could provide the opportunity to walk off some of the calories consumed after eating at all the local eateries. Interacting with the locals, maybe seeing something off the regular tour track, would appeal to many. As I said earlier, you could learn a new language and practice it in a country that speaks that language. There are vacation packages that will help you learn a language *as* you tour their country.

I remember picking up a book and teaching myself a little French when our daughter left for a study abroad program in Europe. I practiced for months and when we finally met her in Madrid at the end of her school year, I was ready to test my newfound skills on the locals. Thankfully, she was fluent in both French and Spanish. I asked questions and made a comment or two wherever we went. I must have sounded authentic because I was responded to in kind. As I sputtered, my daughter came to the rescue.

Because we are very comfortable with the internet, most boomers will do lots of research to seek out special trips with great deals. We won't make the call to book the trip until we've gathered as much information as we can first. When we took that trip to Europe I bought train tickets and booked our hotel stays online. Everything worked out well—there were no glitches because I had done lots of research first.

Many websites cater to traveling boomers. Several suggestions can be found for ways to cut costs and enjoy vacations that educate, too. There are sites that cater to home exchanges, tours that pair wine tasting and culinary classes, even sites that will point you to trips you can make with your parents. Don't forget the services of a good travel agent; they can be a wealth of information.

Gardening

Some boomers have issues: cranky knees, slippery backs, stiff joints, less energy—and *yet*—I can't imagine not enjoying a garden whether it's filled with flowers, veggies, herbs, or a combination of everything. I have fresh bouquets in the house year-round, as flowers are my drug of choice. You might enjoy something more subdued and quiet, maybe something with a Zen feel. Most people like a little private oasis outside.

My flowerbeds have always been filled with perennials because they continue to grow each year. Some of them grow *too* prolifically and vex me as much as weeds! They need to be deadheaded on a regular basis to keep them looking sprightly, or to encourage them to continue blooming throughout the season. Of course it depends on the plant, but I find myself crouched over, scissors in hand more than I would like.

Annuals give more bang for the buck many times, as they are generous with their color and number of blooms. They need to be replaced every year and they, too, often need to be deadheaded for the full effect. Vegetables are usually considered annuals, and have their own tending requirements.

All this work! I've always enjoyed working in my yard even when I'm weeding with the sun on my back. Used to anyway... Time marches on and like everyone, I'm busy. My body isn't as willing to take the abuse of sitting on my knees in the flowerbeds, squatting over plants, yanking and digging, scraping and hauling dirt.

Time to revamp the yard to make it friendlier to the cranky body. I'm doing research, and in the interest of arming the local northwest boomers with some tips to make life more rewarding in the garden, I went to the annual Home and Garden Show. Here are some tips that help.

Marjorie, working the booth at Washington State University Clark County Extension (WSU Extension) says before doing anything - take a minute or two and just STRETCH; it really will help as you begin working.

Consider implementing raised beds. There are several kinds—check the internet. I saw several examples at the show from simple structures to large, artistic boxes that were a focal point in the design of the landscape.

Plant more things in pots; they are actually a raised bed, too. You might want to put those pots on wheels so you can move them around on the patio or deck. I can't count the times I've enlisted my husband's help as we've lugged pots back and forth. With wheels, you'll save your back as you escort them to various spots and rearrange your view. With the gorgeous varieties of pots available, there's no reason you can't create the look you're trying to achieve.

I asked everyone if we can skip the weeds. Nope. Darn. However, we can make the chore a little less daunting. Save your newspapers or even cardboard boxes (flattened). Place your paper (several layers) onto the flowerbeds around your plants. Cover the newspaper with compost (2 to 3 inches thick). This creates a barrier and should help keep the weeds at bay. Those that do come up will be easier to remove. I was told to begin the weeding in late winter and early spring before they seed. They'll be much easier to pull because the ground is so wet. I have found a hoe to be very effective in scraping the weeds off the surface of the soil; this works particularly well when they are small and plentiful.

Try planting ground cover that's thick enough to discourage weeds. Corsican mint and creeping thyme work well and they are more "steppable" should you need to walk on them.

Plant more trees and shrubs. They offer color and structure and don't require as much maintenance. You will still need to prune them occasionally and rake up their leaves in the fall if they happen to land where you don't want them. Sometimes they make good mulch. I am slowly adding things that have good seasonal color and shapely, beautiful "bones" in the winter's garden.

What kind of tools are you using? Find ergonomic tools that can alleviate some of the stress to joints and muscles. I was told to check out the website for Red Pig tools where Bob Denman will have tips and user-friendly, ergonomic tools for you. He is a blacksmith and an inventor; you'll be amazed.

Plan for wider walking paths. One landscape designer, Christine Ellis, of Gregg & Ellis, suggested walking surfaces should be laid with a smooth finished tile rather than tumbled tiles. They will provide a more even surface accommodating walkers and wheelchairs if needed. Smooth finished tiles can be negotiated more easily because they will have even surfaces that avoid the variations in height that some surfaces create. While smooth is good, slippery is not and there should be some sort of traction. She also suggested using one color when you do tile the patio or walkways. Sometimes people have trouble with depth perception and keeping the flooring or walkway one color helps tremendously. If you're planning a natural walking path, visit Scented Acres in Vancouver, Washington where paths are filled with tiny lavender petals and where you can buy lavender in bulk. Can you imagine what a fragrant stroll that would make?

Use drip irrigation and automatic sprinklers if you don't want to stand over your beds with a hose. There *are* times, though, I actually enjoy the mindless peace of doing nothing while I hand water the flowerbeds and pots.

Hire teens and grandchildren to help do the heavy work. I heard that suggestion *over and over again* at the Home and Garden Show! Who knows, you might be helping to cultivate a future gardener.

If you live in the Northwest, here is a list of compatible plants that you may want to incorporate. If you live elsewhere, I'm sure there are lots of local books and resources for you to peruse.

This should help ease boomers into a more carefree gardening venture. This is certainly not a complete list and isn't evenly weighted by variety. You would do well to consult the Western Garden Book. It is a wonderful resource.

Trees:
    dogwood (Cornus Kousa)
    smoke tree (Cotinus coggygria)
    Japanese snowbell (styrax japonicus)

Shrubs:
    heavenly bamboo (nandina domestica)
    rhododendron (Ericaceae)
    azaleas – once established
    blueberry (Vaccinium)
    mock orange (Philadelphus coronarius)
    (old-fashioned) heirloom roses (Rosa)
    dappled willow (Salix integra 'Hakuro Nishiki')
    lavender (Lavandula)
    hostas (Hostaceae)

Plants:
    Solomon's Seal (Polygonatum biflorum)
    black-eyed Susan's (rudbeckia hirta)
    coral bells (Heuchera)
    foamflowers (tiarella)
    bellflowers (campanula)
    coneflowers (Echinacea)
    jasmine (jasminum)
    rosemary (Rosmarinus)
    fern (too many genus names)

And Then There's Body Shaping

For me it started early. The twins were born when I was twelve. I named them Thunder and Thigh and just like American Express™, they don't leave home without me. In my 40's, they made some new friends, The Flying Squirrels. When I hold my arms out, you can see where they live— they droop from my arms between the shoulders and elbows. I see they've sent invitations to the Bulge Brats who keep asking to hang around at my waist. I guess my whole body is becoming a party and I think it's being held somewhere below my knees. Gravity is in charge. Maybe I can learn to walk on my hands for the next 50 years. That should just about bring things back where they should be, don't you think?

Body shaping and pulling, erasing, nipping, tucking, removing, contouring... The list goes on and boomers are listening, as they seem to be attuned particularly to the changes in their bodies for many reasons.

In a society that worships youth and a youthful appearance, we find ourselves trying to keep up with appearances, too. We want to look the part because we _feel_ more youthful. Sometimes there's a little denial going on—did you do a double take when you passed a mirror wondering who that older person could possibly be?

Sometimes it's easier to snag that job if you look younger. First impressions count, as we've learned over the years. People will use these adjectives to describe you: energetic, enthusiastic, confident, knowledgeable, capable, and youthful, in great shape—if you look and act younger.

It takes money to invest in anti-aging tricks that revive that person in the mirror who _used_ to look back at you a few years ago. I've done a little investigating for you. _Okay_, for me, too.

Not wanting to rely only on the internet, I made appointments for a free consultation at two different body contour establishments. I had several questions and they had several answers, of course.

By adding everything up on their lists, in order to regain *my* youthful glow and appearance, I would need to write a check for $22,320. I would also need to rob a bank! My mom taught me a long time ago to accept myself. I'm trying...

If *you* want to recapture your youth, albeit for a short time, I'll give you the highlights. All it takes is money and courage! I always worry about jinxing myself. My health is good; should I risk it for a procedure that isn't technically necessary?

One category, the injectable, will give you a quick fix for instant gratification. This is where you'll find Botox™. It takes about a week to see the effects. It will take care of those crow's feet and what is called "the 11's" on your forehead—the frown lines between your eyebrows. The results will last about three to four months. The length of time it lasts depends on your metabolism. I was told it takes 25 units of Botox to correct crow's feet and about 50 units to correct the "11's" or 50 units to do some work on your neckline where the "necklace" wrinkles form. At one of the establishments I visited, it cost $10 to $14 a unit. Do the math.

Another category of corrections includes the fillers. These will give you an instant fix. This group includes products such as Restylane™ and Juvederm™, and Perlane™. I was told one vial would correct wrinkles above the upper lip. Fillers usually last from six to 12 months. Side effects can include bruising and swelling from somewhere between 24 hours to two days. The cost I was quoted was $500 for one vial. These products have what is called hyaluronic acid in them, which is a natural substance found in skin.

Intense pulsed light (IPL) is another option. I'm told this is where a beginner to cosmetic enhancement should start. IPL is *not* a laser treatment. One quote I got for the first treatment for the face costs $349. Of course, you need three treatments for the full effect (why is it *never* one treatment?). Three treatments can cost from $1440 to $2400 at one establishment I visited. You can have a treatment and go right back to work. You are cautioned to protect your skin from the sun. IPL can remove things like fine lines, freckles, wrinkles, acne scars, blemishes and large pores. It lasts about a year.

More magic falls under the category of laser treatments, and there are several varieties and treatments out there. There is a skin-tightening laser, used to help the skin on the face and neck with the best results seen three to four weeks after treatment. The results last one to two years. Three treatments for the face and neck cost $2400, but there are sometimes specials bringing the cost down to $1440 at one establishment. For six treatments to the rest of the body, you're looking at $3,600.

There are Smoothbeam™ laser treatments that reduce acne, fine lines and wrinkles. They do some tightening of the skin. Sometimes this treatment is combined with another for results that are more defined.

You may have seen the television ads for Zerona™, a form of cold laser and low-level laser treatment. This type of laser reduces inches and is non-invasive. I was told you don't necessarily lose weight after treatments, but you will lose inches if you follow their guidelines. Online, I found this average cost: $2,329. It lasts unless you gain weight. The fat cells that were "emptied" during the process will fill up again if you do!

Another very popular and permanent way to lose fat is with Lipodissolve™, an injected treatment. This process is not for someone who needs to lose a lot of weight. It could be useful for the person who has areas of fat that never seems to go away. The fat cells "explode" with this process, I was told. It is non-invasive, but requires several treatments. I was quoted a price of $600 to $800 per treatment. Your chin, for example, would require three treatments and your body would require six treatments (for each area). There is a two-week time lapse to see the results with some bruising and swelling in the areas that were treated.

With ANY of these magical treatments, I would do everything I could to educate myself before considering any of them. It is best to read lots, get several opinions from professionals, and remember who you are talking with when you ask. I know there are many reputable businesses offering these services with very positive results, or they wouldn't be so popular, but remember whom you are talking with and do your homework.

A friend told me she has the perfect solution for all of her wrinkles. She said if she sees a new wrinkle, she just eats one more cookie to fill it. Ha!

I'm a chicken; maybe Mom *is* right. I wonder how long I can accept what I look like (and camouflage the rest) before I start looking into the possibilities again. Then, too, I really *couldn't* rob a bank!

For that Warm and Fuzzy Feeling

Two of my clients have a kitty. One client owns a beautiful Burmese cat. She is able to take care of her cat as long as I provide the supplies needed. We go together to take her kitty to the veterinarian's office once a year. Hilda has always owned a Burmese cat and can't imagine what she would do without her companion.

With my help, Sally got her kitty three years ago from a cat adoption place. Sally lives in a retirement community. She was told she wouldn't be able to have a cat. The staff was concerned she would not be able to manage the care for it. They were right; she would not have been able to manage the day-to-day upkeep of a cat, at least not without a little fore-thought. I put parameters in place by helping to secure extra paid help who would come in to clean the litter box and make sure there was always plenty of food and water in her dish. I also asked that they take some time to play with the cat for a few minutes to assure a little exercise because Sally was limited physically. Today, they make a very cute "couple" and adore each other.

The benefits of owning a pet are many for all of us, but I think especially for people as they get older. The physical contact is comforting. The love and affection given and received is something we all need. For some whose family is scattered or non-existent, pets provide the family that is missing. Loneliness is very serious among seniors especially.

A pet can help ease the way when someone finds himself or herself sud-denly without a spouse. Furry companions can help combat depression. They ease grief, pain, and fear. They create lots of laughter and joy for their owners. They calm and soothe many a weary heart. Physically, they help lower blood pressure. As their focus is redirected on their pets, peo-ple tend to forget their own problems.

81

There is a sense of purpose when one needs to get up and get moving to let a dog outside or to dole out food a couple times a day. Fido forces his owner to get a little exercise, too, thereby building muscle and making the blood pump a little faster.

How many times have pets been a great conversation starter? They can create an opportunity to make new friends. Sometimes people will approach someone new if that someone has their furry friend with them. Owners may live longer, healthier lives if they share their home with an animal.

If it isn't possible to own an animal, there are organizations like Therapy Pets, and Delta Society, who provide animals that spend time interacting with people. More and more, pet therapy is recognized as a legitimate tool in nursing homes, hospitals, prisons, and mental-health institutions. Animals chosen to be therapy pets must be gentle, affectionate, and immune to sudden or loud noises.

Once our kids left home, I found my attention refocused on our cat. The cat is my baby and she satisfies that nurturing feeling that makes me all warm and fuzzy inside. She comes down the stairs to greet us when we've been out. Every evening, she wants to sit in my lap and gaze into my eyes with her motor running to let me know how much I mean to her. I've always been amazed at how much people and animals need each other and can become true friends. Syrupy, yes? Bet you're right there with me, though.

The Empty Nest

We raise our children to be independent and to move on with their own lives. We experience their leaving home in bits and pieces as they go off to college, to work or to live independently. I remember when our son left for college. In the months and weeks before he left, I found myself unexpectedly tearful when I thought of him leaving. I know I wasn't unique in my reaction thinking of my grown son taking flight. I will say, though, when it was actually time to say goodbye outside his college dorm, I did better than I thought I would. It didn't hurt that his sister was still around to fuss over for a few more years, and in some ways it was easier to watch her go off to college.

Then we celebrated another of life's defining moments. I felt the same wistfulness when we watched our daughter marry. She was so beautiful and her husband most handsome; we couldn't have been more proud. I realized our little girl was gone forever. Realistically she had been for a long time but this was proof she is truly her own entity now. We rejoiced with her in the promise of their future, but I knew we would still miss the charming little girl, the busy excited teenager we once sheltered.

For me, the hardest thing to realize was that we are not central to their lives anymore. I missed the fact we were no longer a part of their *every* day. They don't call us *first* to share the events of their lives. They socialize with their friends more than they do with us. This is the way it's supposed to be—I *know* that, and that's the way I want it. That doesn't keep the house from echoing with the silence that is more common now. We have a wonderful relationship with each of them and are happy when we do all get together. I'm not trying to paint a sad picture here. Anyone with children faces this transition. We're not done transitioning—no one is ever finished! There are grandkids to look forward to, and more things to become involved with every year, and more pets to adopt. I found I just needed to *reinvent* myself after being so focused on our children. I'm finding it exciting, interesting, fulfilling, and joyous.

My advice is to find the new *you*. If you are having trouble letting go or are trying to decide what to do now, here are a few suggestions.

If you're married, refocus on your mate; plan some date nights, recapture the romance and the intimacy you knew when you were a young, childless couple. Remember?

You could certainly host an exchange student and turn your attentions to them. Think of all the information and knowledge you could pass on to them!

Adopt a pet. If she could tell us, I'm sure our poor cat would tell you she gets a little too much attention. Reread the previous chapter.

Volunteer as hosts for youth groups. Teach them some of your skills or hobbies. Find a community service project in your area and volunteer your time.

Make a new friend—or two or three at one of the retirement communities in your area. I never cease to be amazed at the lives people have led and your attention and friendship couldn't be more welcome. Many times families can't provide for all their needs. Make yourself available for a chat, a small favor, a special occasion, or take them out for a meal. The benefits to everyone are enormous.

Investigate a new interest. Read about it and see if you want to delve further into it. Travel. Visit friends and family you haven't had time to see.

You'll find yourself back in the thick of things and that lonely, quiet nest will fill once again.

Losing Your Job Before You're Ready

Being thrown off track by finding *yourself* downsized unexpectedly is too common these days. You still have kids in college or you're still putting money away for retirement. You need the medical insurance that goes along with the job.

I don't think losing one's job carries the level of shame and embarrassment it did even five years ago. We remember the days companies were loyal to their employees and vice versa. We felt secure. By all indications, it would seem those days are over. It's a new world.

Though I'm certainly not a career counselor by any stretch, I have a few thoughts that will help you jump start your next position.

If you're struggling with depression, please do yourself a favor and get the professional help you need. It will make a big difference in managing the hill you need to climb for that next position.

Having a well-polished resume is a given, no matter what. If you need help writing or updating yours, get it. This is the first impression you give to a potential employer; make it polished and professional. With so many folks out of work, posting your resume online randomly isn't going to be as effective. Companies that receive hundreds or thousands of resumes and applications can't possibly respond to most of them. If you *do* apply online, follow up to be taken seriously, though you still may not get a company response.

It's true—it's often about timing and/or who you know. Get dressed as professionally and as appropriately as possible and get yourself to some networking groups. Visit chamber of commerce events. Let people know you're looking for work, but spend most of your time investing in relationship building. Develop a rapport with people who attend. Most chamber of commerce groups will let you visit a few times before they require you to buy a membership. Take advantage of that fact. Offer to help with functions or group projects if you can. Find out what other networking groups attendees belong to and visit those if possible. You'll be taken more seriously as a job candidate with marketable skills if you've become a familiar face. You'll hear firsthand about new job openings.

Volunteer your time in programs that hold your interest for another opportunity to build relationships with people. Once people get to know you and observe your work ethic, they'll be happy to recommend you for positions that open.

Join LinkedIn, an online business social network. It costs nothing unless you decide to buy their more in-depth program. This is a great way to post your resume and your background. Get in touch with others you've worked with in the past, get recommendations, and let people know you're looking for opportunities. Join groups in LinkedIn that pertain to your field of interest or past positions. Join the discussions within those groups to keep your name out front. Add updates to your profile.

Position yourself as an authority in your field of work by writing articles, or posting on your own blog.

Visit trade shows that pertain to your line of work. Have business cards with you. Even if you aren't currently working, you can still print cards with basic information; never go *anywhere* without them.

Meet colleagues for coffee or lunch to let them know you're looking. Always be dressed appropriately for the position you are hoping to get. It gives people the right impression—that you are serious and working hard at finding a position. When you look like you're ready to dive right in, you're halfway there.

Continue to keep active and busy; then tell folks what you've been doing. You don't want anyone to think you haven't done much with your time since you last held a position.

You might consider starting your own business. There is a lot of planning and strategy but the rewards are wonderful and you get to be in charge. It takes time to build your own business and depending on what type of business you want to start, you may or may not have a lot of overhead or startup expense. Do your homework.

I have started two businesses and have found both to be rewarding. My knowledge base has grown extensively, making me more marketable should I decide to work for another company someday.

Live Zestfully and Fully

I polled a few of my clients. I asked them what they know now that they wish they'd known when they were in their 50's.

> Save lots of money.
> Money isn't everything.
> Take the time to smell the roses.
> Life goes faster the older you get.
> Life moves slowly when you don't feel well.
> Don't wait; do what you want to now.
> Be flexible.
> Don't take life so seriously.
> Live and let live.
> Stay positive.
> Find a reason to look forward to each day.

I feel very positive about the future. I believe we're in control of that future more than ever and in more ways than would seem possible. Follow the tips and guidelines I've given you and I think you'll agree. Please do your own investigating, too. Life is good and there *is* actually more to look forward to in those golden years than my client thought (intro).

Helpful Links

FabCab™ | Seattle WA | **www.fabcab.com**

An example of additional housing for an aging parent

http://www.metlife.com/mmi/about/index.html?WT.ac=GN_mmi_about

National Council on Aging
http://www.ncoa.org/

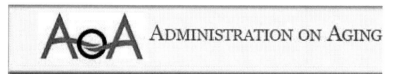

http://www.aoa.gov/AoARoot/Index.aspx

National Institute
on Aging ■ ◆ ✳ ❋
LEADING THE FEDERAL EFFORT ON AGING RESEARCH
http://www.nia.nih.gov/

Helpguide
A trusted non–profit resource
www.helpguide.org

AARP
http://www.aarp.org/

http://nasmm.org/

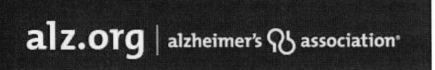

http://www.alz.org/index.asp

http://www.eldercarematters.com/

About the Author

Marilyn conceived the idea for **There For You** several years ago and was able to bring it to fruition in January 2005. Her background has provided her with knowledge and experience as she deals with the issues of aging in a sensitive manner.

Before creating **There For You**, Marilyn was the marketing director for an adult retirement community, where she interacted with residents and staff on a daily basis. She felt a need to reach out and help families who were struggling to find the time to get everything done.

As an advocate and consultant for baby boomers as well as elder adults, Marilyn has become a trustworthy friend to the many who rely on her expertise as she helps them find solutions to the issues they live with every day. Marilyn believes aging for today's boomers will be vastly different than it is for their parent's generation.

There For You creates an outlet for families who need an extra hand as they try to balance work and family and caring for elder parents. In addition to being a consultant, she provides a wide range of services for her clients by running errands, escorting and attending medical appointments, coordinating necessary moves. She helps by offering solutions to lifestyle changes, organizing outings, facilitating pet care, and especially by providing companionship.

As a busy culinary arts instructor, Marilyn created her first business, **Cooking Capers** in 1990 and wrote a cookbook titled, *Marilyn's Ginger 'N' Jazz.* She continues to enjoy cooking and baking today.

She relished being a guest on "The Patsy Swendon Show," (South Texas' KTSA Radio; 3-hour live radio program) doing cookbook reviews, interviews, and restaurant reviews, as well as being a guest on "A Couple of Cooks," (KENS-TV: CBS affiliate in San Antonio, TX).

Marilyn is an avid gardener with a keen eye for floral design. Additionally, she has a flair for interior design, creating warm, inviting spaces. Read her blog for more insight and information and to enjoy her other topics as she shares some of her varied interests.

She and her husband live in Wilsonville, Oregon. Their son and daughter already *know* what to expect from their parents in the coming years…

Dear Marilyn:

Thank you for entrusting your book into my hands and heart. I feel very fortunate to have been granted the opportunity for an early peek at it— and I find it very charming, entertaining, and informative. You certainly have a good grasp of the many topics faced by the boomers for themselves as well as their aging parents.

I found myself nodding, sighing, cringing, laughing… all the while gleaning new ideas, putting old ideas into perspective, and wondering if you will be there when I need you!

Nancy Doty, Guardian/Conservator
Nancy Doty, Inc.
Portland, Oregon

To order additional copies, go to www.ThereForYouToo.com
Or to www.MarilynSlaby.com